$a^2+b^2=c^2$

THIS BOOK BELONGS TO:

_____

THIS BOOK IS DEDICATED TO ALL THE TEACHERS AND FUTURE TACHERS.

Copyright © 2024 Grow Grit Press LLC. All rights reserved. No part of this book may be reproduced in any form without permission in writing from the publisher. Please send bulk order requests to info@ninjalifehacks.tv

Paperback ISBN: 978-1-63731-948-2
Hardcover ISBN: 978-1-63731-950-5
eBook ISBN: 978-1-63731-949-9

Printed and bound in the USA.
NinjaLifeHacks.tv

Ninja Life Hacks®
by Mary Nhin

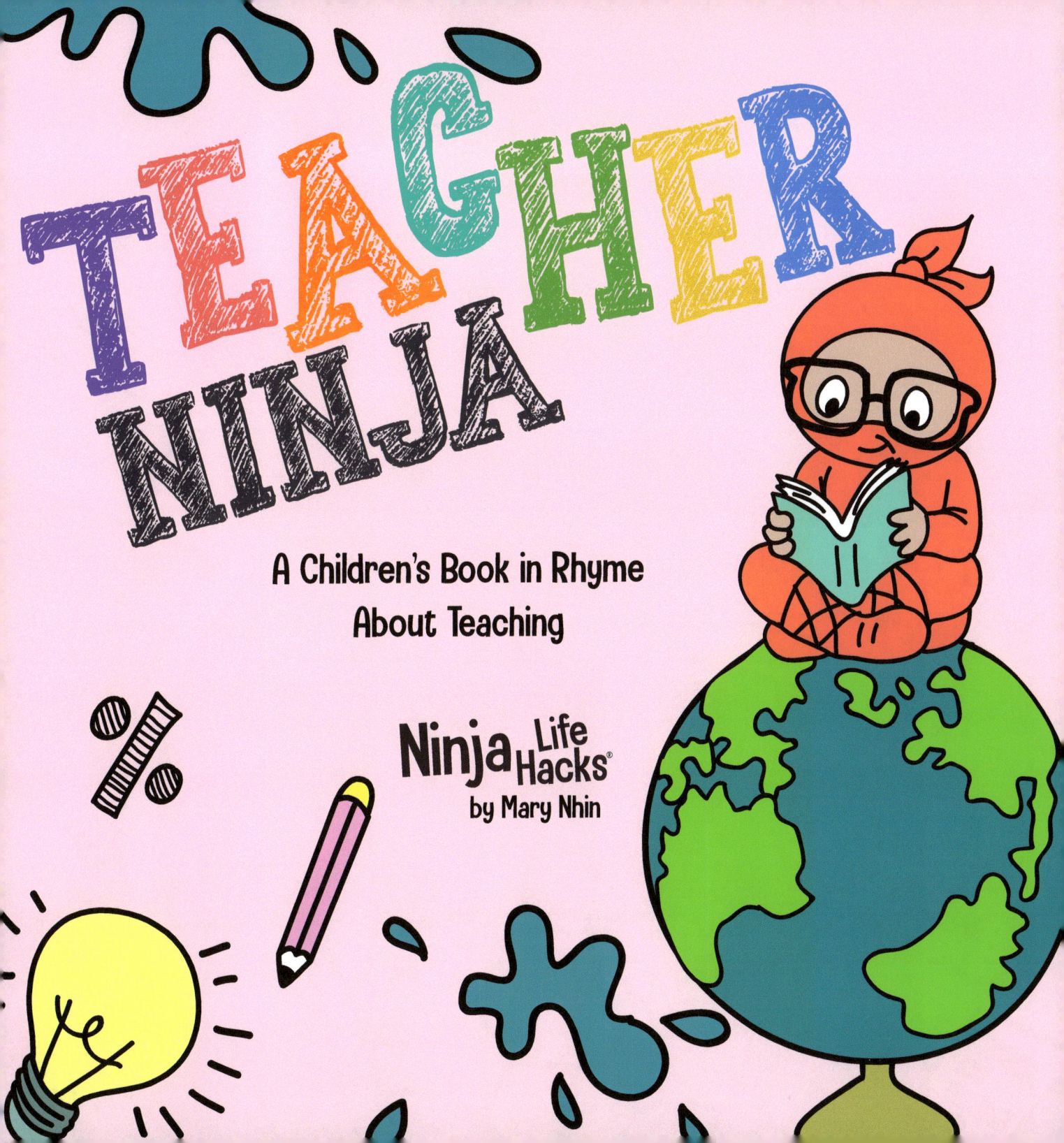

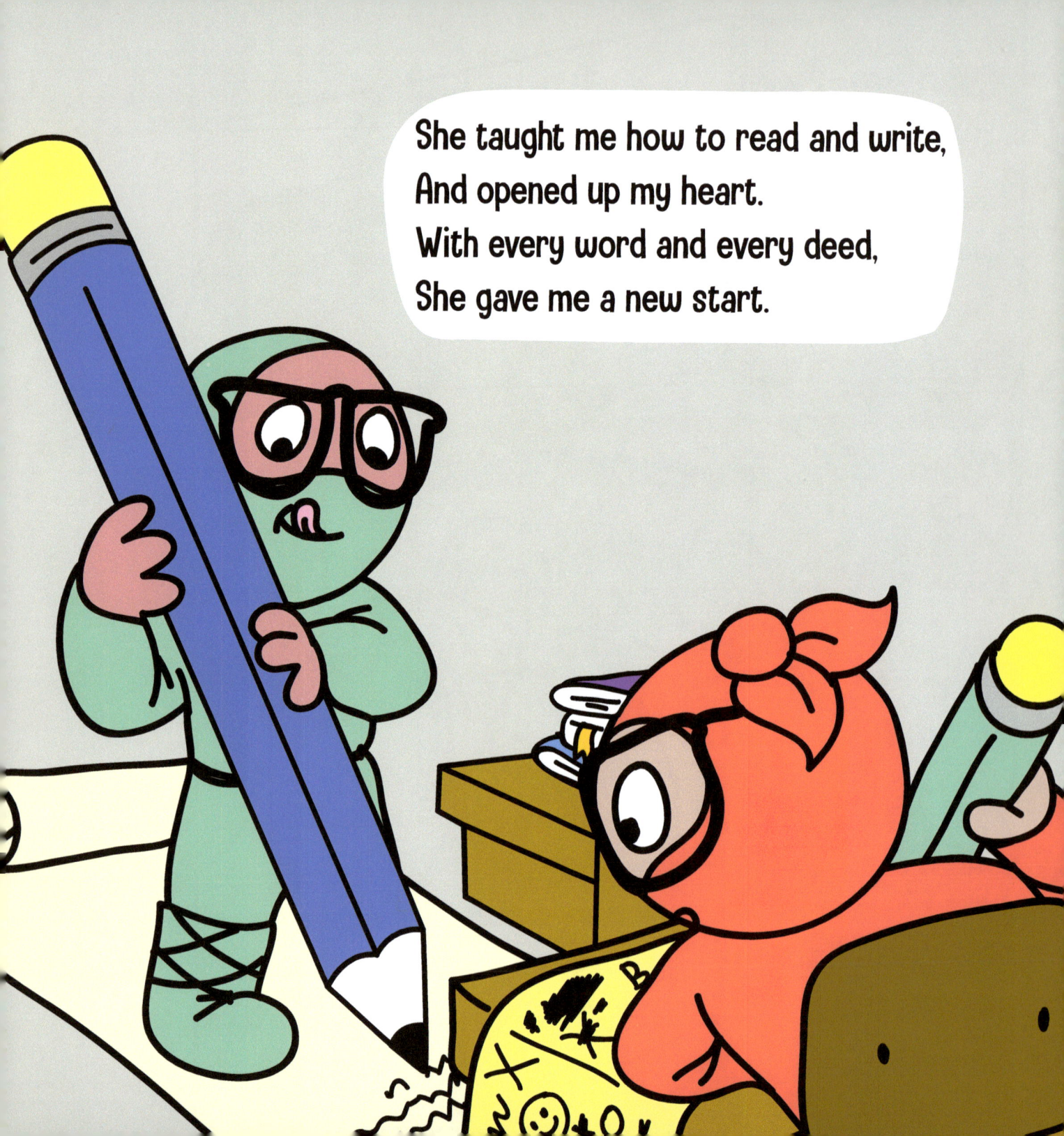

She wasn't just a teacher, no,
She was a guide and a friend.
She showed me paths I hadn't seen,
With lessons that never end.

> As the years rolled on, I hit some bumps,
> With challenges to face.
> But when I felt lost or unsure,
> Her wisdom I'd embrace.

$1+2=3$

$13-4 \times 9=?$

$7 \times 8 = 56$

$27/3=$

$/4$ of

$36+24$

$4444/11=$

$2/6$ of $30=$

$(-4)+16+(-12)$

$38-(-24)-22=$

$(8 \times 2)-(60/5)=$

$(12/4)-(-3 \times 9)$

$[(18/3) \times (6/3)]$

$(\times 7)+$

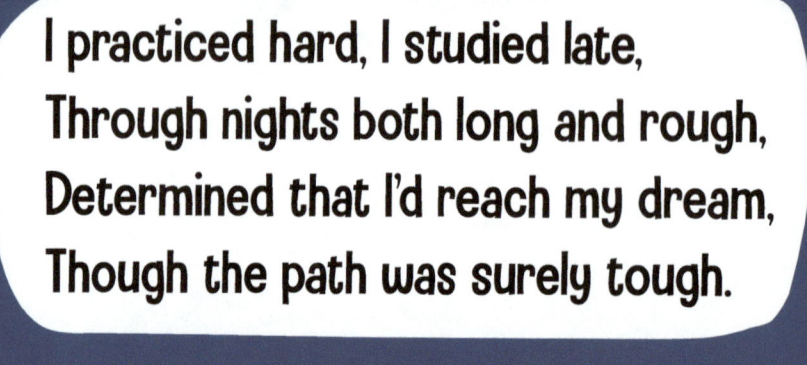

I practiced hard, I studied late,
Through nights both long and rough,
Determined that I'd reach my dream,
Though the path was surely tough.

I teach them not just numbers and words,
But how to be their best,
To face the world with courage,
And how to pass life's tests.

When they ask about my dream,
And what teaching means to me,
I tell them that my greatest joy is helping them
To be what they were meant to be.

I love to hear from my readers. Email me your feedback or thoughts on what my next story should be at info@ninjalifehacks.tv

Yours truly, Mary

 @marynhin @GrowGrit
#NinjaLifeHacks

 Mary Nhin   Ninja Life Hacks

 Ninja Life Hacks

 @officialninjalifehacks

www.ingramcontent.com/pod-product-compliance
Lightning Source LLC
Chambersburg PA
CBHW041712160426
43209CB00018B/1815